DIVING AND SNORKELING GUIDE TO

The U.S. Virgin Islands Second Edition

St. Croix, St Thomas, and St. John

Susanne and Stuart Cummings

Pisces Books
A division of Gulf Publishing Company
Houston, Texas

Acknowledgments

We would like to express our appreciation to the following companies and individuals whose extreme generosity with their time, assistance and cooperation was invaluable to the preparation of this guide:

Chris Sawyer Dive Center, St. Thomas
V.I. Divers Ltd., St. Croix
American Airlines
Hotel Caravelle, St. Croix
Stouffer Grand Beach Resort, St. Thomas
Hyatt Virgin Grand Resort, St. John
Bob Kirkpatrick, U.S. Virgin Islands Dept. of Economic Development and Agriculture
Mark Thomas, Development Counselors International
Arlene Stevens, U.S. Virgin Islands Division of Tourism

We extend a very special thanks to Chris Sawyer, owner of Chris Sawyer Dive Center in St. Thomas, and Jimmy Antoine, owner of V.I. Divers in St. Croix, whose abundant and unparalleled knowledge of their local dive sites is reflected throughout the pages of this guide. We'll be back to dive with you both soon!

Library of Congress Cataloging-in-Publication Data

Cummings, Stuart.
    Diving and snorkeling guide to U.S. Virgin Islands / Stuart Cummings, Susanne Cummings. — 2nd ed.
    p. cm.
    Rev. ed of: Diving and snorkeling guide to the Virgin Islands / by Stephen Bower, Bruce Nyden, and the editors of Pisces Books.
    Includes bibliographical references (p.) and index.
    ISBN 1-55992-053-X
    1. Skin diving—Virgin Islands of the United States—Guide-books.
    2. Scuba diving—Virgin Islands of the United States—Guide-books.
    3. Virgin Islands of the United States—Description and travel—1981— Guide-books. I. Cummings, Susanne. II. Bower, Stephen, 1947- Diving and snorkeling guide to the Virgin Islands. III. Title.
GV840.S78B635   1992
797.2'2—dc20   91-35695
                                        CIP

Pisces Books
A division of Gulf Publishing Company
P.O. Box 2608, Houston, Texas 77252-2608

Printed in Hong Kong

10 9 8 7 6 5 4 3 2 1

Table of Contents

Publisher's note: At the time of publication of this book, all the information was determined
to be as accurate as possible. However, when you use this guide, new construction may have
changed land reference points, weather may have altered reef configurations, and some
businesses may no longer be in operation. Your assistance in keeping future editions up-to-date
will be greatly appreciated.

Also, please pay particular attention to the diver rating system in this book. Know your
limits!

A diver experiences the exhilaration of exploring the crystal clear waters of the U.S. Virgin Islands.

How To Use This Guide

This guide is designed to acquaint you with a variety of the best and most popular dive sites in the U.S. Virgin Islands and to provide useful information that will help you decide whether a particular location is appropriate for your abilities and intended dive plan, e.g., macro vs. wide-angle photography, drift dive, wall dive vs. shallow reef dive, etc. In Chapters 3 and 4, you will find a dive site by dive site description of the special features of individual sites and information regarding recommended skill levels. The experience levels are repeated in a condensed format at the beginning of these chapters.

Regardless of how you choose to use this guide — either reading it from cover to cover or selecting sections of interest — certain chapters should be viewed as required reading. Chapter 5 on "Smart, Safe Diving" is of primary importance. No matter how much we think we know or remember, we can always benefit from a refresher. And the section on "Reef Etiquette and Buoyancy Control" in Chapter 5 focuses on tips on how to help preserve our fragile marine environment and be ecologically responsible divers. We hope you'll find that some of the tips in this section will help you make a personal contribution to preserving our fragile reef system, as well as make you a more skillful diver. If you plan to keep diving into your senior years, wouldn't it be nice to have something beautiful to look at?

A diver inspects one of the many colorful wrecks around the U.S. Virgin Islands.

1

The underwater adventures of the U.S. Vigin Islands come in all shapes and colors — some even look like sea dragons!

Although this guide is directed at people who enjoy spending a substantial amount of time in or under the water, everyone has to come up for air. And because some surface intervals are longer than others, we have tried to give you a brief overview in Chapter 1 of the U.S. Virgin Islands on dry land. The gist of it is quite simple: You can eat every meal in a different restaurant, stretch out on a different beach, visit a different landmark and shop somewhere new every day of your vacation and you still wouldn't run out of things to do and places to see. If you have been to any of the U.S. Virgin Islands, you obviously enjoyed your stay enough to consider returning. But don't imagine that just because you've seen one, you've seen them all. If you have never experienced these islands, get ready for a great time . . . underwater and topside.

The Rating System for Divers and Dives

Our suggestions as to the minimum level of expertise required for any given dive should be taken in a conservative sense, keeping in mind the old adage about there being old divers and bold divers but few old bold divers. We have rated the dive sites based on the following qualifications: A *novice* diver is in decent physical condition and has recently completed a basic open-water certification diving course by an internationally recognized certifying agency, or is a certified diver who has not been diving recently (within the last 12 months), or is a certified diver who has no experience in similar waters. An *intermediate* dive is a certified diver in excellent physical condition, has been diving actively for at least a year following a basic open-water course, and has been diving recently (within the last 6 months) in similar waters. An *advanced* diver has completed an advanced certification diving course, has been diving recently in similar waters, and is in excellent physical condition.

If you are not sure which category you fit, ask the advice of a local divemaster or instructor on the island. You will find a list at the end of this guide of all the dive operators on each island. They are best qualified to assess your abilities based on the prevailing dive conditions on any given site. Be honest about your qualifications — diving "over your head" can be an unpleasant and uncomfortable experience. If you're still in doubt, ask a divemaster or instructor to accompany you on the first dive in new waters.

If you haven't been diving for 12 months or more, you and your equipment may need a checkout. Make sure your equipment, especially your regulator, is in top condition. If your skills are a little rusty or you are using new and unfamiliar equipment for the first time, take a refresher dive in the pool with your local dive store or do one when you arrive in the islands with an instructor at the dive center with which you'll be diving.

1

Overview of the U.S. Virgin Islands

A thousand miles southeast of Miami and only 18 degrees north of the equator lies America's own Caribbean paradise — the U.S. Virgin Islands. Consisting of St. Thomas, St. John, and St. Croix — the major centers of population and commerce — as well as 50 islands, cays, and rocks jutting from the sea, the U.S. Virgin Islands belong to the Lesser Antilles chain, which separates the Atlantic Ocean from the Caribbean Sea.

History

Christopher Columbus discovered these islands in 1493 on his second voyage to the New World. He was so overwhelmed by their pristine beauty that he called them "The Virgins," a reference to the tale of St. Ursula and her 11,000 virgins whose incredible beauty was legendary.

The next 150 years was relatively uneventful with a series of unsuccessful attempts by the English, French, Spanish, and Knights of Malta to establish permanent settlements on the islands, punctuated by the colorful activities of pirates and buccaneers who sought a safe haven. In 1672, the Danish West India Company firmly established its presence in St. Thomas, and in 1694 in St. John. In 1733, purchasing St. Croix from the French, they united all three under Danish dominance and transformed the islands into one of the major sugar producers in the region.

It was not until the Civil War that the U.S. first recognized the strategic importance of these islands with their fortresses and deep-water harbors, but the senate failed to approve the purchase of St. Thomas and St. John from Denmark for $7.5 million. At the outbreak of World War I, when the islands became critical to U.S. control of the Caribbean basin and the Panama Canal, the purchase was finally consummated for a mere $25 million in gold.

The U.S. Virgin Islands remained under the jurisdiction of the U.S. Navy for the next 14 years, when the U.S. Department of the Interior assumed responsibility for them. Home rule was granted in 1970. In the 1950s and 1960s, the popularization of air travel brought an influx of

ST. THOMAS

ST. JOHN

Miami

Bahamas

ATLANTIC OCEAN

Jamaica

Puerto
Rico

CARIBBEAN SEA

SOUTH AMERICA

U.S. VIRGIN ISLANDS

ST. CROIX

tourists to the islands, significantly altering the basis of their economy. Today, the islands are an incorporated territory under the U.S. flag. The official language is English. The currency is the U.S. dollar. In fact, the only thing U.S. citizens from the mainland may have to adjust to is driving on the left hand side of the road.

Geography and Climate

Iguanas and turtles, exquisite reefs and lush seagrass beds, luxurious resorts, historic ruins, world-class dining and first-class shopping, combined with perfect weather and warm, clear waters attract about 1.8 million tourists every year. Year-round temperatures average between 77° and 82° F thanks to the steady trade winds from Portugal. Water temperatures vary only a few degrees, ranging from the mid-70s in the winter to the mid-80s during the summer.

Unlike many Caribbean islands, which are flat and arid, the U.S.V.I.'s are lush and colorful. Each is dramatically sculpted with mountainous terrain — the highest elevations reaching to 1,500 feet on St. Thomas' Crown Mountain, 1,277 feet on St. John's Bordeaux Mountain, and 1,165 feet on St. Croix's Mount Eagle — endless powder white beaches, low coastal plains, and verdant tropical rain forests. Yet, despite these similarities, each possesses its own strong physical and cultural identity.

St. Thomas, the busiest and most commercialized of the three islands, and St. John which is the smallest, quietest and least developed, are situated adjacent to one another. Both lie between the Atlantic Ocean and the Caribbean Sea. St. Croix, the largest island, is located 32 miles to the south and lies completely in the Caribbean. It is separated from the other two by an ocean trench that plunges more than 12,000 feet to the seafloor.

The ruins of more than 100 sugar plantations can be seen all over the countryside in St. Croix.

The first glimpse of St. John that visitors enjoy is beautiful Cruz Bay where the ferry from St. Thomas docks.

Local Information and Services

Currency. The U.S. dollar is the official monetary unit.

Time Zone. The U.S.V.I. observe Eastern Standard Time when the mainland is on Daylight Savings Time. The time in the islands is one hour earlier during the winter when the mainland is on Eastern Standard Time.

Postal Service. The U.S. Postal Service handles the mail so first-class letters are $.29 and postal cards are $.19.

Telephone Service. Local phone calls between the U.S.V.I. are $.25. Long distance rates to the mainland are surprisingly low.

Banks. Although some U.S. banks have branches in the U.S. Virgin Islands, don't expect them to cash your stateside check, even if you have an account at the same bank back home. Hours are approximately the same as on the mainland.

Drake's Seat is one of St. Thomas' most famous landmarks and offers one of the island's most breathtaking views.

Credit Cards. Major credit cards are accepted at most, but not all, places. It is a good idea to check whether your hotel or restaurant takes the cards you carry before you arrive.

Car Rental. To rent a car, you must show a U.S. driver's license and a credit card. A reservation is recommended, especially during high season. Your U.S. driver's license is valid for 30 days. *Remember that you drive on the left.*

Electricity. Electricity is the same as on the mainland (110-120 volt/60Hz). No plug adaptors are needed.

Tourist Information. For more information, contact the U.S. Virgin Islands Division of Tourism nearest you. Tourism offices are located in Atlanta, Chicago, Los Angeles, Miami, New York City, Washington, D.C. San Juan, St. Croix, St. John, St. Thomas, Toronto, and London.

Shopping. Even in the days of pirates and smugglers, the U.S. Virgin Islands were considered a sort of shopper's paradise where you might pick up goods that had been forcefully removed from an unfortunate merchant ship on the high seas at bargain prices. Today, shopping is still one of the big attractions in these islands. In fact, many visitors go *just* for the shopping, because the duty-free shopping quota is twice that of any other destination in the Caribbean.

Transportation. The U.S. Virgin Islands are very accessible. Several major airlines fly between U.S. gateway cities and the international airports in St. Thomas and St. Croix. Cruise ship arrivals account for nearly twice the tourists as air traffic, docking either in St. Thomas Harbor at Charlotte Amalie or the Frederiksted Pier in St. Croix. For island hopping, commuter carriers and charter services are available at the airport.

Customs and Immigration. U.S. citizenship is sufficient for entry into the U.S. Virgin Islands. You don't need a passport, visa, inoculation, or voter registration card to enter. However, you do need a form of positive identification upon your departure, because so many visitors stop in the islands on their way to the U.S. from some other destination.

St. Croix

St. Croix is the largest of the three major U.S. Virgin Islands. Three times larger than St. Thomas, its diverse terrain ranges from arid lowlands and sheer rugged cliffs to mountains and a rain forest. It was the last of the three islands to come under Danish control, but reminders of a strong Danish influence are evident all over the island in the architecture and the ruins of over 100 sugar mill plantations that dot the countryside. The two main population centers — Christiansted and Frederiksted — offer visitors a perfect blending of modern amenities and services with old world ambiance.

Government House is one of Christiansted's reminders of its illustrious Danish history.

The Hotel Caravelle, which is nestled on the harbor's edge in Christiansted, St. Croix offers an abundance of hospitality, charm, and convenience for guests seeking a downtown location.

Christiansted. Most of the hotels and resorts are located in or near Christiansted. Founded in 1734 by the Dutch West India Company, it is a quaintly picturesque harborside town that still retains much of its original charm from the 1700s, when it was a crown colony of Denmark and one the Caribbean's key ports. In 1952, the area near the wharf was designated a national historic site and many of old homes and public buildings have been preserved and restored. Because the area is quite concentrated, a short walking tour will include most of the major landmarks. Many of the old buildings in Christiansted conceal beautiful inner courtyards and arcades which are well worth exploring.

Frederiksted. Situated on the waterfront on St. Croix's west coast, Frederiksted's architecture differs from that of Christiansted because many of the original Danish structures were destroyed either by a huge tidal wave in 1867 or a fire in 1878. Restoration efforts are underway to return the historic authenticity to the area. In and around town, you can visit forts, plantations, botanical gardens and the Cruzan Rum distillery. If you have time for nothing else, try to catch one of Frederiksted's spectacular sunsets from the pier or a waterfront cafe.

Beaches. St. Croix's beaches have been ranked among the world's most beautiful. Slivers of ivory sand that fade gently into cobalt waters rim the island. Davis Beach is so ideal a tropical beach that it was used

Shoppers can find a wide variety of high-quality merchandise from designer clothing to jewelry in Christiansted's many shops.

as the setting for the final scene in the film, *Trading Places*. Because it is part of Carambola Resort, you must sign in at the gate, but you'll find some of the best snorkeling about 100 feet offshore of this beach, so its worth the extra effort. But no matter where you happen to be, you won't be far from a beautiful beach on St. Croix. Most are located on the east coast and along the north shore and many offer some beach facilities, equipment rentals and refreshments.

Sightseeing. Buck Island tops the list of tourist attractions. It is accessible only by boat, and several watersports operations in Christiansted run snorkel, dive, and picnic excursions to Buck Island daily. Beyond Christiansted and Frederiksted, St. Croix's points of interest are scattered around the island and you may want to rent a car or moped to do your touring. It's a good idea to plan your trip in advance and get explicit directions to your destinations. The roads are good, but they are poorly marked and it is easy to miss a critical turn-off.

Shopping. Like her sister islands, St. Croix is a shopper's haven offering competitive prices on everything from crafts and clothing to liquor and jewelry. You'll find a good selection of brand names at low prices. Most of the shopping in Christiansted is on King Street, Company Street, and Strand Street, which are lined with fine boutiques and quality goods. There are also quaint shops in Frederiksted. Local tourist

11

magazines that are available in all of the hotels will provide detailed information on where you can buy what.

Restaurants and Nightlife. Dining options are numerous and varied. In general, the cuisine is excellent, the portions substantial, and the service professional and friendly. Fresh seafood appears on every menu, but you'll also find very good Italian, Caribbean, and continental fare as well.

After dark, there is always something happening. You just have to look for it. The locals will be happy to steer you to the best place to watch the sun set, listen to some music, dance the night away, or try the limbo.

Accommodations. St. Croix has it all — large resorts with 18-hole championship golf courses near town, intimate resorts off-the-beaten track, downtown hotels on the harbor, and condos. The local hotel association can provide information and guidance on available accommodations on the islands.

Transportation. The best way to see St. Croix is by car. They can be rented at the airport upon arrival or your hotel can arrange one for you. Taxis are available but they can get pricey. They are unmetered and rates are posted in the vehicle, but it is a good idea to agree on the fare before departing for your destination.

The downtown wharf area in St. Croix's Christiansted has been designated a national historic landmark.

St. Thomas

When it comes to attracting tourists in the U.S. Virgin Islands, St. Thomas wins hands down with more than a million people visiting each year lured to its shores by its warm waters, beautiful beaches, gorgeous weather, exceptional sports facilities, world-class resorts and restaurants, and duty-free shopping. Although it is more commercialized than St. John or St. Croix, St. Thomas has managed to retain much of its old Danish charm as well as a few reminders of its days as a haven for pirates and gunrunners.

There is plenty to see and do on this island from watersports and sunbathing to exploring castles, forts, or Danish relics.

Charlotte Amalie. Nestled on the waterfront and surrounded by three steep hills, Charlotte Amalie is one of the most picturesque towns in the Caribbean. It is also one of the finest deep-water harbors, a popular port for cruise ships, and home to one of the largest bareboat and crewed charter boat fleets in the world. Shopping is unparalleled and, for non-shopping enthusiasts, there are plenty of historic landmarks to visit in town that can be enjoyed on foot.

Charlotte Amalie in St. Thomas overlooks one of the finest deep-water ports in the Caribbean.

Charlotte Amalie in St. Thomas is a labyrinth of alleys and passageways lined with quaint boutiques and shops where great bargains abound.

Shopping. To many tourists, St. Thomas is synonymous with shopping and it deserves it reputation as the bargain center of the Caribbean. From luxury imports to island souvenirs, St. Thomas has just about anything you could desire. Most hotels also have boutiques with souvenirs as well as high-quality resort wear, but your best buys are along the main streets in town and the alleys, mini-malls, and narrow passageways that create a labyrinth of stores.

Sightseeing. Although for many visitors, shopping is sightseeing, there are many fascinating points of interest beyond the stores. Charlotte Amalie is known for its fortresses, castles, historic buildings, and architecture as well as its spectacular harbor views. Other panoramic vistas not to be missed include those from Drake's Seat and The Mountaintop of beautiful Magen's Bay, which *National Geographic* magazine named as one of the world's ten most beautiful beaches. With one of the largest commercial charter fleets in the Caribbean, you can also see the islands by powerboat, sailboat, bareboat or crewed, take a day sail to St. John, cruise to the British Virgin Islands by ferry, or enjoy a glass-bottom boat ride or a romantic sunset cruise.

Beaches. More than 40 lovely beaches fringe St. Thomas, providing picnic tables shaded by palm trees, watersports equipment for rent, restroom facilities, restaurants, and bars. Some even have campgrounds should you decide to travel on a budget. Wherever you decide to spread your beach towel, don't leave your valuables in an unlocked car or unattended on the beach. This is just as much a paradise for thieves as for sunbathers.

View from the Mountaintop of Megans Bay on St. Thomas, which was named one of the ten most beautiful beaches in the world by National Geographic *magazine.*

The world-class Stouffer's Grand Beach Resort on St. Thomas' east coast offers visitors the ultimate in luxury and service.

Dining and Nightlife. Fine restaurants are a trademark of St. Thomas. Menus range from continental cuisine with a Caribbean twist to oriental fare. But the best part of the dining experience is the tropical ambiance, which also sets the mood for nightlife on the island. Entertainment abounds in Charlotte Amalie, as well as at the hotels and resorts, and ranges from piano bars, dance clubs, and shows to limbo demonstrations and contests, quadrille dancers at poolside, and calypso, jazz, and steel bands.

Transportation. In St. Thomas, you can rent a car, jeep, or scooter and enjoy the island at your own pace. One caution — traffic jams are not unusual on this bustling island. Try to avoid driving cross island at rush hour and be prepared to spend a little time finding a parking space in Charlotte Amalie. A wide variety of island tours are available and private taxis will transport you to your destination efficiently as well. Commuter airlines operate among nearby islands for island hopping and the ferry between St. Thomas and St. John departs from Charlotte Amalie and Red Hook continuously every day.

St. John

From the moment you set eyes on the picturesque sailboats dotting the harbor at Cruz Bay, you know that this island is special. Only 19 square miles in area, St. John may be the smallest of the three main U.S. Virgin Islands, but it is, in many ways, the most captivating.

At one time, it was inhabited by thriving plantations and companies exporting sugar and rum, whose merchant ships filled Coral Bay and Cruz Bay. In the 1950s, American financier and multi-millionaire Laurence Rockefeller discovered St. John as he cruised the Caribbean on a six-year voyage. Falling in love with the perfect white beaches and spectacular views, he purchased almost half the island, built a secluded resort and

The Annenberg Plantation Ruins on St. John date back to 1733.

The luxury Hyatt Virgin Beach Resort overlooks beautiful Smith Bay and offers a full complement of watersports activities.

campgrounds on the site of an old sugar plantation, and donated the remaining 5,000 acres to the government. Today, two thirds of St. John is preserved as national park. The exquisite, uncrowded beaches that rim its shores, its pristine waters and shallow reefs, miles of hiking trails, and the unspoiled, uncommercialized beauty of its mountainous landscape clearly distinguish St. John from its busier neighbors.

Beaches. If there is one thing St. John does not lack, it is world-class beaches such as Trunk Bay, which features a marked snorkeling trail, Cinnamon Bay, Hawksnest Bay, and Maho Bay. Many of the beaches provide shower and changing facilities as well as refreshment concessions. Those located nearer to Cruz Bay tend to be more crowded, but if you want to find someplace more secluded and private, rent a car explore the beaches along the north shore.

Sightseeing. When you arrive in St. John, you might want to pay a visit to the National Park's Visitor Center in Cruz Bay. Park rangers are happy to orient visitors and provide information on the island's flora, fauna and history. The rangers also conduct a number of interesting programs including snorkel trips, hikes along the park's 20 miles of marked trails, and craft shows. A visit to the Annenberg Plantation Ruins on the northern coast which dates back to 1733 and features an old sugar factory building and windmill should be on everyone's itinerary.

The roads on the island are often steep and curvy but they are in good condition for the most part. The coastal road from Cruz Bay offers numerous scenic way points that offer breathtaking views down onto Trunk Bay, Hawksnest, Cinnamon, Cruz Bay, and Coral Bay.

Transportation. There is no airport on St. John. If you haven't chartered your own boat, the most effective way to get there is to hop the ferry that runs continuously between St. John and St. Thomas. Once

17

Virgin Islands National Park

If you've traveled to many islands in the Caribbean, you may wonder how this tropical paradise has escaped the bulldozers of developers and the overcrowding of eager condominium seekers. Over the years, little has changed to alter the island's inherent beauty. The reason is simple — 56% of St. John is preserved as national park. Traveling to St. John by ferry — there is no airport — you can enjoy its pristine sheltered beaches, cruise or snorkel its clear offshore waters, hike along scenic marked trails, vacation at well-maintained campgrounds, visit the ruins of an old plantation, or rediscover ancient stone carvings. The National Park Service conducts regularly scheduled tours and talks given by the park rangers. And, thanks to them, St. John remains an exquisite jewel in the Caribbean.

Two-thirds of St. John is national park and will remain unspoiled and undeveloped.

you're there, it is easy to get around. The best way to see St. John is to rent a car or jeep and tour the island at your own pace. You can also take a "safari bus" into the park and learn about the island from the knowledgeable guides.

Shopping. Shopping in St. John is relaxing and low-keyed. Cruz Bay is filled with quaint boutiques worthy of browsing. Small shops sell high quality goods from exclusive resort wear to original hand-crafted jewelry and ceramics. Mongoose Junction has a few shops where local artists

Trunk Bay, the most famous beach in St. John, attracts visitors with its marked underwater snorkel trail.

Mongoose Junction's complex of quaint shops and restaurants offers original arts and crafts and fine dining.

and crafts people display some very unusual and lovely work. At the Hyatt Virgin Grand Resort, you also find some high-end shops with excellent quality tropical wear for sale.

Accommodations. St. John's accommodations are more limited than on the other islands, but you will find some truly world class resorts here. For the more budget minded, there are also intimate guest houses and cottages, as well as some excellent campgrounds at Cinnamon and Maho Bays.

2

Diving the U.S. Virgin Islands

Between the three main islands of the U.S. Virgin Islands, it would take a lot of bottomtime to cover all of the good diving that surrounds them. However, that isn't a problem, because consistently favorable wind and sea conditions make these islands diveable year-round.

Temperatures in the islands are fairly consistent throughout the year. Ranging in the winter from about 82° F during the day to 70° F at night, temperatures rise only about 4-5° F during the summer months. Cooling breezes provided by constant trade winds temper the climate so that it rarely gets uncomfortably hot.

Tropical showers are a common occurrence but they are short and refreshing and rarely interfere with leisure activities. As prevailing winds change from northeast in the fall to southeast in the summer, they diminish and bring calmer seas and clearer water. From April to August, seas are calm and visibility can exceed 100 feet, but beware of hurricane season, which intensifies during the latter part of the summer. Late summer and early fall are predictably damper with rain resulting in some silt run-off and reduced water clarity.

The water temperature ranges from the mid 70s to the mid 80s depending on the season. For divers planning to do multiple dives, a light wetsuit or shorty is recommended. A diveskin will not provide thermal protection but will minimize potential scrapes and abrasions from coral.

Diving Conditions

Diving conditions in the Virgin Islands are somewhat predictable. Two- to three-foot seas with sporadic white capping tend to be the rule. Occasionally, more often during the winter, ocean swells of up to five to eight feet are caused by low-pressure areas moving through. Even when the waters seem too rough too dive, diveable sites can always be found in the islands' lee.

Although you may encounter a formidable current in a few areas where tidal action play a role, that tends to be the exception rather than the rule. Pillsbury Sound, which lies between St. Thomas and St. John, is the

Divers will discover an abundance of healthy marine growth on the U.S. Virgin Islands' many wrecks.

most likely place to encounter a significant current, but on the occasions when tidal movement makes this area hazardous for divers, there are alternative areas nearby that are well protected. Local dive guides will routinely check out the current conditions and inform divers of any existing currents. If you plan to beach dive on your own, find out what the prevailing conditions from a local dive store or other divers. If there is a current — light or heavy — remember to begin your dive swimming into the current.

Because the Virgin Islands are a U.S. territory, dive operations are subject to U.S. standards and regulations. Dive boats must meet U.S. Coast Guard approval, skippers must be licensed by the U.S. Coast Guard, and all dive guides are instructors or divemasters certified by an internationally sanctioned U.S. certifying agency. All of this maximizes the safety of your diving experience. There are complete medical facilities on each of the islands. Recompression chambers are located on St. Thomas and only a half-hour away in Puerto Rico. In addition, the islands maintain Coast Guard search and rescue teams as well as air evacuation services.

Dive operators will most likely want to see your C-card and sometimes even your log book before they take you diving, so don't forget to bring along both.

3

Diving in St. Croix

Diving in St. Croix is exceptionally diverse. There is near-shore and beach diving, walls, reefs, pinnacles, wrecks, and one of the most spectacular pier dives in the Caribbean.

When Hurricane Hugo decimated the island in September 1989, it was feared that the effects on the marine environment would be devastating. To everyone's relief, the reefs and walls suffered very little damage and remain remarkably healthy, colorful, and exciting.

The preservation and protection of the marine environment, however, is an on-going concern for St. Croix's dive operators. In early 1991, they joined together to launch Project Anchors Away. Recognizing that the coral reefs daily suffer from anchor damage caused by anchors and chains being dragged across the reefs, participants in Project Anchors Away installed 20 permanent moorings on St. Croix's most popular dive sites. This not only protects the reefs, but also makes access to the sites easy and convenient for divers.

Permanent moorings installed on popular dive sites in St. Croix protect the fragile reefs from boat anchors.

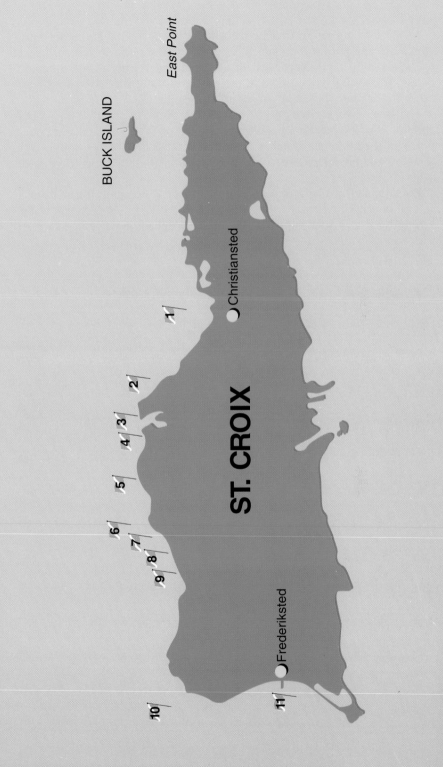

BUCK ISLAND

East Point

○ Christiansted

ST. CROIX

○ Frederiksted

Map key: Flag = dive sites
          Snorkel = snorkel sites

(See next page for Dive Site Ratings.)

Most of diving off St. Croix occurs along its substantial northern shore, which stretches from the spur and groove reef system of Scotch Banks to the six-mile Long Reef west of Christiansted Harbor to the dramatic drop-offs of Salt River Canyon, Cane Bay, and Davis Bay to the northwest tip of the island where the wrecks of Butler Bay lie.

First-rate dive services are available and most of the dive operators and hotels offer excellent packages that include diving and accommodations. Full equipment rental is available at most dive stores, and prices for new equipment purchase are very reasonable and competitive with stateside prices.

Buck Island also offers scuba sites, but dive operators must have a special concession license to take divers to the island. Several local water sports shops and dive operators run regularly scheduled dive and snorkel trips to this national marine park.

Dive Site Ratings

	Novice Diver	Novice Diver with Instructor or Divemaster	Intermediate Diver	Intermediate Diver with Instructor or Divemaster	Advanced Diver	Advanced Diver with Instructor or Divemaster
1 The Barge		x	x	x	x	x
2 Little Cozumel		x	x	x	x	x
3 East Wall of Salt River Canyon			x	x	x	x
4 West Wall of Salt River Canyon			x	x	x	x
5 Rust-Op-Twist		x	x	x	x	x
6 Jimmy's Surprise				x	x	x
7 Cane Bay Drop-Off		x	x	x	x	x
8 West Palm Beach		x	x	x	x	x
9 Northstar Wall			x	x	x	x
10 Wreck of Butler Bay			x	x	x	x
11 Frederiksted Pier	x	x	x	x	x	x

Typical Depth Range:	75-90 feet
Typical Current Conditions:	Little or none
Expertise Required:	Novice with instructor or divemaster
Access:	Boat

When you descend the mooring line onto this sunken barge which lies near the channel off Long Reef, you may not be overly impressed with the visibility, which suffers because of its proximity to the harbor opening. And you may not be overwhelmed by the coral growth on this vessel. But you will be treated to a delightfully warm welcome by a substantial and enthusiastic fish community.

The Barge, which was sunk intentionally to attract marine life, lies overturned along a slope in 60-90 feet of water. Local dive operators have been fish feeding at The Barge for sometime and, as a result, divers are invariably greeted by dozens of fish looking for a handout. If your dive-master has brought some edible treats on this dive, you can expect to be joined by large numbers of coneys, yellowtail, black durgeons, Nassau and tiger groupers, barracuda and horse-eye jacks.

This is an excellent site for fish portraits as you won't have difficulty finding suitable subjects. In fact, you might even convince the resident green moray. And, although this site is not renown for its coral growth, the Barge is surrounded by hard corals that provide shelter for a number of spotted morays who may be persuaded to pose for you!

One of St. Croix's dive operators moors his dive boat on one of the permanent buoys that have been installed on the dive sites.

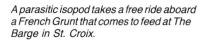

A parasitic isopod takes a free ride aboard a French Grunt that comes to feed at The Barge in St. Croix.

Little Cozumel   2

Typical Depth Range:	40-70 feet
Typical Current Conditions:	Light to none
Expertise Required:	Intermediate
Access:	Boat

To the east of Salt River Canyon is a delightful dive site called Little Cozumel. The highlight of Little Cozumel are two adjacent mini-walls that begin at 40 feet and drop vertically to 65-70 feet. A rocky sand chute separates the walls, which are situated about 50 feet apart. Occasionally swept by cleansing currents that show off the marine growth at its best, Little Cozumel's walls are adorned with pretty soft corals, sea fans, sea whips, and sea plumes that create a picturesque underwater scene.

At 65 feet, an undercut probes deeply into the wall for about 20 feet. The underside of the overhang is heavily encrusted with red and orange sponges. The undercut offers an excellent photo opportunity as snappers, groupers, and jacks congregate here. If you want to be assured of the best fish shots, be sure you're one of the first divers to reach the undercut before other divers have had a chance to frighten them away.

In general, the whole area is well populated by a prolific marine community of goatfish, angelfish, barracuda, whitespotted filefish, grouper, and various species of snapper.

The mooring is set just west of the walls but the swim is short and easy.

V.I. Divers owner, Jimmy Antoine, explores one of the mini-walls at Little Cozumel. ▶

Divers can easily swim beneath the overhang at 65 feet on Little Cozumel in St. Croix.

Typical Depth Range:	40-130 feet
Typical Current Conditions:	None to light
Expertise Required:	Intermediate
Access:	Boat

Only a short boat ride from Christiansted is Salt River Canyon, which features two distinctively different dive sites — the East and West Walls. Although they are just across the chasm from one another, the distance is too great to see them on the same dive.

The East Wall of the canyon is the more precipitous and in some opinions the more dramatic of the two with its gradual slope from the crest to the point at which it curves to the east along the northern coast. The coral rubble slope begins fairly near the shore and gradually becomes more precipitous. The East Wall begins as shallow as 37 feet and as deep as 45 feet, where a mini-wall slopes off at a 40° angle. The wall occasionally drops more sharply, but generally it slopes more gradually to 1,000 feet.

A coral-encrusted "pinnacle" marks the mouth of Salt River Canyon. Nearby deep-water gorgonians, tube sponges, orange elephant ear

A wide variety of tube and rope sponges provide a dramatic accent of color on the East Wall at Salt River Canyon.

Healthy deep water gorgonians are plentiful on the East Wall at Salt River Canyon.

sponges, and black coral trees accent the wall with vibrant color. At 120 feet, unusually pink-hued black coral trees grow to an impressive size.

The water is usually fairly clear with visibility reliably around 60 feet. Equally reliable are the schooling fish that cruise the wall. In fact one of the features that makes this site special is the abundance of fish. You are likely to see big-eye creole wrasse cruising the rim of the canyon as well as squirrelfish, black durgeons, blue runners, and blue chromis. On the deeper slope, small schools of blackbar soldierfish cruise among the smaller coral heads and gorgonians. Barracuda are common in the area due to the abundant supply of food in the form of schooling reef tropicals. They tend to watch visiting divers from a distance, although curious by nature, they will often move in for a closer look at these strange marine creatures. Some lucky and alert divers have even spotted a manta at this site, so be sure to pay attention to what is around you — above as well as away from the wall.

For those who may be familiar with the Hydrolab Project owned by the National Oceanic and Atmospheric Administration (NOAA), which had been located in Salt River Canyon since 1978, the four-man underwater habitat is no longer here. The project was removed in 1990 and moved to Virginia where scientists will continue their research.

Typical Depth Range: 40-130 feet

Typical Current Conditions: Usually light but can exceed 2 knots when high swells are present

Expertise Required: Intermediate to advanced depending on weather

Access: Boat

Salt River Canyon is a former submarine canyon located off Columbus Landing. Its two walls begin in 25 feet of water and slope vertically to over 1,000 feet. Although they are situated only 1,500 feet apart, they offer two very different dive experiences.

The West Wall of Salt River Canyon is possibly the best known dive area on the island and has been one of the most popular dives for years. The West Wall starts at about 40 feet and plunges almost straight down to 150 feet where it joins the canyon bottom. This vertical descent is impressive as the coral species vary with their depth along the wall.

Brilliant purple tube sponges and deep-water gorgonians can be found all over the face. If you enjoy photographing black coral trees, on this dive you'll find them as shallow as 80 feet, and at 120 feet you'll discover a black coral forest.

Visibility averages about 60 feet unless high seas churn the waters and reduce the clarity. Under normal conditions, the rim of the wall is visible from the surface.

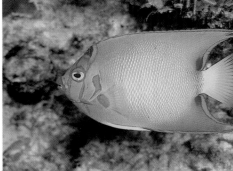

Salt River Canyon, once a submarine canyon, features two unusual wall dives on either side of its plunging chasm.

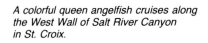

A colorful queen angelfish cruises along the West Wall of Salt River Canyon in St. Croix.

Christiansted has been rebuilt since the ravages of Hurricane Hugo, but still retains its old world charm and architecture.

Hurricane Hugo

In September 1989, Hurricane Hugo swept through the U.S. Virgin Islands with winds exceeding 200 miles per hour. Surprisingly, St. John suffered only marginal damage. St. Thomas was hit much harder. St. Croix which received the brunt of the hurricane's violence was devastated as the storm left little in its path but ruin. With a hefty helping of outside assistance, a rainy season in Fall 1990 that boosted the refoliation of the islands, and a lot of hard work and cooperation on the part of local residents, these islands have been rebuilt and are more beautiful than ever before.

Rust-Op-Twist 5

Typical Depth Range:	70-80 feet
Typical Current Conditions:	None to moderate
Expertise Required:	Novice with instructor or divemaster
Access:	Boat

Sandwiched between Jimmy's Surprise and Cane Bay Drop-off is a very pretty spur and groove coral formation called Rust-Op-Twist. It derives its unusual name from a Danish sugar plantation on shore of where the site is located. Just under the mooring, the depth on the reef is 35 feet. Near the mooring are long pipes held down by thick cables

At Rust-Op-Twist cables and pipes serve as a reliable underwater navigation aid for divers.

Lobsters in hiding at Rust-Op-Twist occasionally venture out of their shelters to scavenge for food.

that resemble a railroad track but, in fact, lead to the former shrimp farm on the island. These pipes provide an reliable underwater navigational aid for divers on this site, and are covered with a nice amount of coral growth.

Gradually, the reef slopes at a 40-45° angle to a vertical wall at about 110 feet. All along this incline, hard corals form the foundation for deep-sea gorgonians, lavender-hued sea fans, and graceful rope sponges that sway rhythmically in the slight current. Vivid accents of color are provided by soft corals and purple tube sponges. Holes and small crevices often shelter turtles and lobsters. Eagle rays are even spotted with some regularity on this site.

The excellent color and variety of marine life at this site is fed by currents that flow across the reef. Note the direction of the current from the mooring to the site. Always begin your dive into the current and ride it back to the boat at the end of your dive. If, for some reason, you need to make your return swim against it, make sure you start back to the boat with sufficient air for the slightly more energetic swim.

Jimmy's Surprise   6

Typical Depth Range:	60-90 feet
Typical Current Conditions:	Moderate to heavy current
Expertise Required:	Advanced
Access:	Boat

This is considered an advanced dive because the current from the mooring to the site as well as on the pinnacle can get heavy. But it is this heavy and fairly reliable movement of water that contributes to the excellent visibility — 100 to 150 feet plus — and makes this one of St. Croix's most exciting dives.

Jimmy's Surprise is a pristine pinnacle that rises from the ocean floor at 95 feet to 60 feet. At the base, it is approximately 70 to 80 feet in diameter. There is frequently some current on this site which, although usually manageable, is enough to assure excellent visibility and a plethora of filter feeders all over the seamount. Particularly striking are the beautiful deep-water gorgonians that generously decorate the western side of the pinnacle and the large barrel sponges that surround the coral formation. Small barrel sponges emerge between the gorgonians and brightly colored

Rock beauties swim in and out of the coral nooks and crannies on Jimmy's Surprise in St. Croix.

A steady flow of water nourishes the healthy marine growth on Jimmy's Surprise in St. Croix.

red and orange encrusting sponges complete the tapestry. Jimmy's Surprise seems to be as much a favorite of the local fish as of the divers with a healthy population of black durgeons, coneys, small Nassau grouper, rock beauties, blue and brown chromis, and French angels. At the base of the pinnacle is a small ledge where you might just find a resting nurse shark.

Fish portraits and wide-angle photo opportunities are excellent on this site.

This pinnacle is incredibly clean and healthy. To preserve the beauty of the site, the mooring on Jimmy's Surprise is located away from the pinnacle itself. It's a relatively short swim to the site from the boat and well worth the effort. This is a site you will want to explore more than once!

Typical Depth Range:	5-40 feet to wall; 40-below 130 feet on wall
Typical Current Conditions:	None to light inshore, light to moderate on the wall
Expertise Required:	Novice inshore, intermediate on the wall
Access:	Beach or boat

A half-hour drive west of Christiansted, Cane Bay, one of St. Croix's prettiest beaches, is the shore entry for Cane Bay Drop-off, which lies about 100-150 yards off the shore. If you like beach diving, this is one of the best beach dives on the island. Local dive operators run both boat and beach diving trips to the site as well.

Cane Bay Drop-off is part of the reef and wall structure that parallels the northern shore for about four miles. The wall dive is similar to Northstar. If you beach dive Cane Bay Drop-off, there is parking along the road at Cane Bay. There is likely to be some surf, but you can find breaks where calmer water allows you to wade safely through the coral reef. Because you want to have sufficient air to explore the wall, you might want to conserve air on the swim out by snorkeling a good portion of it on the surface. Swim it leisurely — there is plenty to see on the way. Everything from sea urchins, damselfish, wrasses, sea fans, and

Vibrantly colored encrusting sponges and Christmas tree worms decorate the reef and wall at Cane Bay in St. Croix.

Cane Bay is one of St. Croix's loveliest beaches as well as an easy entry point for an excellent beach dive.

small soft corals inhabit the shallow inner reef. As these coral gardens slope toward the wall, parrotfish, trumpetfish, sand tilefish, tobaccofish, and small turtles appear, joined by black durgeons as you reach the lip of the wall and deeper water.

When you drop down to the rim of the wall, which lies at 40 feet, you will see a spur and groove formation where sandy areas separate large coral heads displaying plate and brain coral decorated with delicately shaped vase and tube sponges in which minuscule gobies as well as larger blue chromis, fairy basslets, damselfish, and sergeant majors play. Soft corals and invertebrates such as anemones, Christmas tree worms, featherdusters, and banded coral shrimp dot the coral heads, while morays hide in the nooks and crannies.

On the wall in the deeper water, divers are joined by bar jacks, eagle rays, spadefish, and a rare but occasional shark. Since Hurricane Hugo churned up the water in 1989, several old anchors have been uncovered.

If you are beach diving and want to do the swim underwater, remember to head back to shore with adequate air and bottom time. If you are diving on a boat, a permanent mooring sits directly on the crest of the wall.

West Palm Beach 8

Typical Depth Range:	35 feet to depth
Typical Current Conditions:	Little to none
Expertise Required:	Novice
Access:	Boat

Situated between Cane Bay Drop-off and Northstar is West Palm Beach, aptly named because it lies directly off of a beach that had been lined by palm trees before a hurricane inadvertently removed them.

At this site, a spur and groove reef formation comprising sculpted coral heads and alleyways leads to the lip of the vertical wall that begins in 35 to 40 feet of water. Descending in a sloping angle to 50 to 60 feet, the wall then plunges steeply far deeper than you can explore on scuba. The upper portion of the wall that is accessible to sport divers, however, is lushly adorned with brilliant orange elephant ear sponges, delicate lacy black coral trees, large seafans, angular antler sponges, and entwining rope sponges as well as a variety of hard corals.

Distinctive butterflyfish are commonly seen at West Palm Beach in St. Croix.

A diver carefully stays off the reef while examining a cluster of rope sponges at West Palm Beach in St. Croix.

Fish life here is abundant. You'll find all varieties of angelfish, occasional groupers as well as spot fin, foureye, and banded butterfly fish, which mate for life and always travel in pairs. This is another site where pelagics sometimes pass by in the deeper waters so you want to look above and around you as you swim along the wall and deeper reef.

Typical Depth Range:	50 to below 130 feet over the wall
Typical Current Conditions:	Light to moderate
Expertise Required:	Intermediate
Access:	Boat or beach

Depending on your preference for boat or beach diving, Northstar Wall is easily accessible from either. The beach entry is possibly the best of the island's beach dives. The entry is a little less than a mile west of Cane Bay. To get into the swimmable water, it is necessary to cross over a coral ledge that has a lot of sea urchins. Exercise caution here, especially if the surf is significant. Sea urchin spines won't penetrate your fins, but if you bump into one, they can be very uncomfortable.

Once you've entered the water, the swim to the wall is about 200 yards from the beach. If the somewhat lengthy swim doesn't appeal to you, Northstar Wall is visited regularly by dive boats from Christiansted who will drop divers directly on the wall.

Northstar Wall begins at about 40 feet and drops to 300 feet. Its illustrious history is told by the anchors scattered along the wall that attest to the one-time presence of distressed ships.

Hundreds of blue chromis like the one pictured school around the reef and near the wall at Northstar Wall in St. Croix.

V.I. Divers boat, Mr. Barracuda, *takes divers to explore dive sites along St. Croix's northern coast daily.*

At about 60 feet, there is sand plateau or shelf in which one large ancient Danish anchor is firmly and permanently embedded. A nearby undercut cavern is usually filled with silversides and above the opening of the cavern is a second Danish anchor.

You can cruise along the wall in either direction and find an abundance of creole wrasses, blue chromis, and damselfish playing among the delicately carved coral formations, small caves, overhangs and ledges. If there is a current, it is a good idea to check the direction of the current and swim into it. It will be easier to return with the current at the end of your dive whether you are returning to the dive boat or to the shore. If you are beach diving, be sure to keep and eye on your air consumption so you have an adequate supply to return to the shore underwater rather than on the surface which is more tiring.

Typical Depth Range: 25 to 65 feet
Typical Current Conditions: Mild to none
Expertise Required: Intermediate with divemaster
Access: Boat

Off the northwestern side of the island near Frederiksted are four wrecks of varying size and depth, all within approximately 100 yards of each other. The wrecks were all intentionally sunk as recreational dive sites.

The 177-foot steel hulled Venezuelan freighter, *Rosaomaira,* is the deepest dive. While being prepared for off-loading, the cargo shifted and she capsized. In April 1986, she was refloated, towed to Butler Bay where the water tends to be calmer than along the northern shore where most of the diving is, and sunk.

The deepest of the four wrecks, she rests in the sand upright in 110 feet of water with her superstructure rising to 60 feet. She is elegantly cloaked in red encrusting corals, pink tube sponges, and an abundance of soft corals. Anemones cling to her bow and huge French angelfish cruise leisurely around the silent structure. Divers will find a variety of photo opportunities on this dive.

Sitting in slightly shallower water at 65 feet, *Suffolk Mae* was a 110-foot steel-hulled North Sea trawler that washed up at Frederiksted during a hurricane in 1984. She now sits upright in the water. Her superstructure was removed before she was sunk and only the hull and deck remain. Its most dominant marine visitors are the schools of horse-eye jacks that cruise around its hull.

Most of the wrecks at Butler Bay can be penetrated safely.

Butler Bay is home to four diveable wrecks that provide excellent photo opportunities and an abundance of marine life.

Nearby, you can dive on the 75-foot ocean tug, *Northwind*. While you may not recognize this little tugboat in its present condition, it was used in the made-for-television movie, *Dreams of Gold*, about Mel Fisher's search for the *Atocha*. The film was shot in Frederiksted and, when the filming was completed, *Northwind* remained in Frederiksted where it was later sunk by Cruzan Divers.

Sitting upright in 50 feet of water, it now is home to a resident turtle, black bar soldierfish, and some eels. You'll find some very good wide-angle photo opportunities using the various parts of the tug boat for background interest.

The fourth and newest wreck is *Virgin Islander,* a 300-foot barge sunk in March 1991 in 70 to 80 feet of water. The last three of these wrecks that lie in shallower water can be dived safely by novice divers accompanied by an instructor or divemaster.

Butler Bay is easily accessible from Frederiksted and the wrecks can be reached in 20 minutes by boat. Christiansted dive operators dive these wrecks frequently and usually schedule it as a morning dive, because the boat ride to the site is about an hour.

A curious diver peers through a sponge-encrusted porthole aboard the 177-foot freighter, Rosaomaira, *which lies at 110 feet in Butler Bay.*

Typical Depth Range:	0-30 feet
Typical Current Conditions:	None to light
Expertise Required:	Novice for day, intermediate for night
Access:	Entry off pier; exit up ladder or at shore

One of the most spectacular dives in St. Croix is off the pier in Frederik-sted . . . especially at night. Frederiksted is situated on the west coast of the island, and although it is the second largest town next to Christian-sted, it has a much larger commercial pier extending 450 yards from the town and in deep enough water to handle the largest of cruise ships. The large sturdy pilings that have supported the pier for so many years are overgrown with exquisitely colored and varied encrusting corals and sponges that provide a safe haven for small marine creatures and inverte-brates. If you like to shoot macro photography, this is a "must" dive.

Amid the pilings, which are densely covered from top to bottom with corals, sponges and small creatures, if you look carefully, you can find orange and brown tube and red boring sponges, red fire and finger coral, dread-red (don't touch this sponge!), iridescent tube sponges, and gray cornucopia. Arrow crabs, brittle stars, banded coral shrimp, Christmas tree worms, featherdusters and big spiny sea urchins are permanent resi-dents at this pier. Near the deeper end of the pier where you make your entry, snapper, grunt, sergeant major, trunkfish, burrfish, trumpetfish, goatfish, and an occasional stingray are likely to swim by. A long-nosed batfish has even been spotted walking on the bottom on its pectoral fins!

A brittlestar clings to a yellow barrel sponge on one of the pilings at Frederiksted Pier.

Although this site is famous for its sea horses — as many as fourteen or fifteen have been found here — you are more likely to see them at night when their natural camouflage is less effective.

While this is a nice day dive, at night it is nothing less than a macro spectacle. At first glance, the dark shapes of the pilings and the remains of discarded "junk" on the bottom create an eerie atmosphere. But, under the artificial light of a dive light, the pilings come alive with color that resembles a modern painting asplash with vibrant primary and pastel hues. On closer inspection, you'll discover a plethora of small marine creatures that emerge with nightfall to explore.

You can easily spend your entire night dive not venturing far from the ladder. And you are certain to run out of air and film before you run out of bottom time.

Clustered on the pilings are a variety of anemones, orange cup tubastrea in with polyps in full bloom and vivid encrusting sponges. Brittle stars, which hide during daylight hours, can be spread out across the same sponges at night. Orange balls anemones unfurl their orange-tipped tentacles at night to pose for photographers. The brown, red, and candy-striped sea horses that you might not be able to find during the day are more visible at night. They tend to be skittish, so if you find one, don't touch it or it might not be there for other divers to enjoy.

Octopus and squid often make an appearance at the pier, and you might find an elusive frogfish perched, almost undetectable, on a patch of encrusting sponge. Stonefish can be found sitting motionless on the bottom while minuscule pufferfish dart around the pilings.

If you enjoy fish portraits, you can get some unusual ones on the pier at night. You can usually get very close to colorful daytime fish as they sleep in their nighttime cocoons.

If you're planning to do this night dive without a local dive guide, you might want to orient yourself to the site by diving it first during the day. At night, it is a good idea to wear a wetsuit to protect you against stings and scrapes that sometimes occur when you bump into a piling or other unidentifiable piece of "junk."

Frederiksted Pier is famous for its seahorses and as many as fourteen have been found on a single night dive. ▶

A variety of different colored tunicates encrust the pilings at Frederiksted Pier.

Patient divers may find an elusive orange ball anemone unfurled at night in Frederiksted Pier.

The most difficult part of this dive is the entry, which is usually made at the wider end of the pier where the water is about 20 feet deep. The easiest procedure is to don your gear at your car and take a giant stride off the pier into the water below. The drop may look a lot longer than the 8 feet plus that it is, but that's because you're eye level adds another 5 feet to that. So get a good hold on your mask and regulator and go for it! If the idea really terrifies you, there is a sturdy steel ladder that descends about 8 feet into the water and you can climb down.

Once you're in the water, you'll find a lot to explore at any depth. However, there can be some surge, which you'll feel less if you stay near the bottom. You'll also see all the interesting creatures that assemble at the base of the pilings. Remember, however, that the bottom is sandy so buoyancy control is critical. Keep a few feet off the bottom and tuck your gauges in your BC pocket. It's easy to kick up the sand and ruin the visibility for everyone else! Be considerate — especially at night!

Exiting can be done at the ladder, but if your swim toward the shore during your dive, you can explore most of the dock pilings and there are several places to exit easily along the way. If you exit along the pier or at the end of it, be aware that the rocks are slippery and some of them may shelter sea urchins, so exit slowly and with caution.

Buck Island Reef National Monument

Buck Island is one of only a handful of U.S. marine national parks and the only U.S. National Monument located underwater. Two miles off the northeast shore of St. Croix, the island was at one time a flourishing forest of 18th-century lignum vitae trees that were harvested and repeatedly burned to enable its insatiable goat population, which was introduced in the 1750s, to graze. The goats, after which the island was named, proceeded to eat everything in sight for about 200 years until they were finally removed. In 1948, the Virgin Islands Government began to administer the island as a park, later transferring it to the U.S. National Park Service. Since then, its natural flora has regenerated and it has become a regular nesting site for the endangered brown pelican.

On the eastern end of Buck Island is its famous underwater snorkeling trail, where snorkelers can see a variety of coral formations and an impressive display of fish that are identified by underwater markers. Although the trail does reveal some wear and tear from human as well as wave damage, it still provides beginners with an opportunity to learn about the coral reef.

Two areas designated for scuba divers lie off the east point. The absence of any current makes it ideal for novice divers. At one site, divers will find a cut in the inside fringing reef where the shallow reef opens out into the forereef area, which lies in about 35 feet of water and features several coral caves that can be explored and an abundance of fish. A second site presents a more generous opening through the fringing reef. The two dive sites are just far enough apart that they cannot be done easily in one dive. Because the openings can be difficult to locate when you return and it is almost impossible to snorkel over the reef because it reaches to the surface, it is important to stay with your dive guide.

Both the snorkel and scuba areas are accessible only by boat so permanent moorings have been installed in both locations in an effort to reduce potential damage to the reef by anchoring.

The National Park Service goes to great lengths to preserve and protect Buck Island's pristine white sand beach and underwater reefs despite fairly heavy visitation. Boat owners need a special license to run trips to the island, but you will find several operators in Christiansted who run daily commercial charters, snorkel and picnic trips, and scuba trips to Buck Island.

4

Diving in St. Thomas and St. John

St. Thomas and St. John offer divers a variety of exciting underwater terrain to explore from deep banks, pinnacles and shallow reefs to coral encrusted wrecks. Beginner and experienced divers will find an ample selection of suitable opportunities with some of the best sites around St. Thomas being 30-foot-deep reefs located within 20 minutes by boat.

Many of the most popular dive sites are equally accessible and frequented regularly by dive operators from both islands. You will find excellent full service dive operations on both St. Thomas and St. John. They offer diving either on a per dive basis or as a package that includes multiple dives and accommodations.

Snorkeling in St. John

There is no shortage of great snorkeling spots along the shores of St. John. According to the National Parks Department, the best are in Hawksnest Bay, Francis Bay, just off Leinster Bay Road, Haulover Bay, Salt Pond Bay, on the north side of Lemon Cay, and between Solomon and Honeymoon Beach.

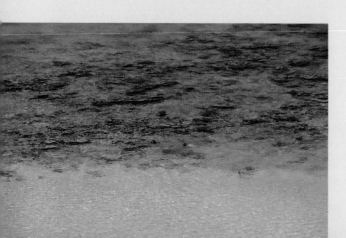

St. John is renown for its excellent snorkeling with shallow reefs easily accessible at most beach sites.

GREAT THATCH
ISLAND

ST. JOHN

Cruz Bay

CONGO
CAY

HANS LOLLIK
ISLAND

THATCH
CAY

GRASS
CAY

Red Hook

LITTLE
ST. JAMES

ST. THOMAS

Charlotte Amalie

BUCK
ISLAND

CAPELLA
ISLAND

FRENCH CAP
CAY

WATER
ISLAND

SABA ISLAND

Map key: Flag = dive sites
Snorkel = snorkel sites

(See next page for Dive Site Ratings.)

There are only a few dive operators on St. John but, unlike St. Thomas or St. Croix, St. John also offers a impressive array of beautiful snorkel sites that are accessible from any one its many beaches. While Trunk Bay's marked snorkeling trail is the most famous, you can obtain an excellent map of the island at the Visitor's Center at Cruz Bay, which clearly indicates where the reefs around the island are located. The park rangers will be happy to point you in the direction of the very best snorkel sites and you can explore them at your leisure. You can also take a boat excursion that cruises around the island, stopping at the prettiest snorkel areas and beaches. This is a great way to see the most of St. John's underwater beauty if you only have one day to spare.

Dive Site Ratings

	Novice Diver	Novice Diver with Instructor or Divemaster	Intermediate Diver	Intermediate Diver with Instructor or Divemaster	Advanced Diver	Advanced Diver with Instructor or Divemaster
1 Carval Rock					x	x
2 Congo Cay		x	x	x	x	x
3 Grass Cay	x	x	x	x	x	x
4 Tunnels at Thatch Cay		x	x	x	x	x
5 Wreck of the General Rogers			x	x	x	x
6 Ledges of Little St. James	x	x	x	x	x	x
7 Cow and Calf Rocks		x	x	x	x	x
8 Capella Island - South Side		x	x	x	x	x
9 Wreck of the Cartanser Senior	x	x	x	x	x	x
10 Deep Ledges at French Cap Cay			x	x	x	x
11 Pinnacle at French Cap Cay			x	x	x	x
12 Saba Island - Southeast Reef			x	x	x	x

The wreck of Major General Rogers *near St. Thomas is one of the most colorful wrecks in the U.S. Virgin Islands.*

Carval Rock 1

Typical Depth Range:	20-70 feet
Typical Current Conditions:	½ knot common, can exceed 2 knots
Expertise Required:	Advanced
Access:	Boat

About four miles northeast of St. John, about halfway between St. John and St. Thomas, is Carval Rock, a dive area visited by dive operators from both islands, weather permitting. On occasion, the currents can be treacherous, which makes the site undiveable, in which case an alternate sight will be chosen. Even on a good day, the current resulting from tidal flow from Pillsbury Sound can be substantial, thereby classifying it as an advanced dive.

In good conditions, this is a site worth experiencing. You have a little bit of everything — dramatic rock formations, coral gardens and a fish community that includes open-water species. Anywhere from 20 to 80 feet, divers are bound to find a host of surprises.

Chris Sawyer Dive Center, one of the oldest dive operations on St. Thomas, has dive centers at the Stouffer Grand Beach Resort and Compass Point.

A brittle starfish tries to find a safe hiding place inside of an orange encrusting sponge at Carval Rock.

Graceful soft corals decorate the ocean floor like a plush carpet. You are likely to find entwining basketstars clinging to them. Through the soft coral garden toward shallower water among the base of the rocks is a passageway. If you follow it to the southwest, you will see two cuts, a small one and then a larger one. If there is not too much surge, it is worth swimming through the second cut to see a dozen or more glimmering tarpon that frequently can be found hovering motionlessly or feeding on schools of silversides on the other side. If there is even some surge, be sure to move through the cut quickly and watch out for the fire coral!

On the northern side of Carval Rock, ravines and sheer vertical precipices covered with encrusting corals and sponges offer some excellent wide-angle photo opportunities. Keep a sharp eye out for manta rays as they fly through the area on occasion.

As a rule, dive boats anchor on south side of Carval Rock. To return to the boat, you can circle the rock or double back over the route you followed to the north side. Your divemaster will likely brief you on the best course to dive. However, watch your air pressure gauge and plan to begin your return with enough air to enable you to swim back underwater as surface conditions are generally choppier on the northern or windward side.

Coral World

The highlight of this fascinating marine park is the three-floor underwater observation tower, one of only three existing in the world. Submerged 20 feet onto the coral reef, its two underwater levels are surrounded by large windows that provide a 360° panorama of the reef and its inhabitants from the smallest invertebrates to sharks and barracuda. The uppermost level of the tower offers a view ranging from offshore islands to the British Virgin Islands and St. John.

It is worth a visit if only to watch the fish feedings, Caribbean reef encounters, and shark feedings that are scheduled daily.

The 4.5-acre park also houses a dazzling aquarium exhibit of exquisite and unusual tropical fish and invertebrates, touch ponds, strolling peacocks, sunbathing iguanas, colorful parrots, duty-free gift shops offering marine-related souvenirs, and a restaurant/bar overlooking Coki Beach.

At Coral World's Pearl Bar, you are guaranteed to find a pearl in your oyster. You can also mail a postcard to friends and family from the only underwater mailbox in the U.S.!

Coral World is open seven days a week from 9 am — 6 pm. The underwater observatory is open three nights a week. Coral World is located on Route 6 at Coki Point in St. Thomas, telephone 809-775-1555.

Coral World, which is located on Coki Point in St. Thomas, is one of only three underwater observatories existing in the world.

Coral World's fish-feedings and underwater exhibits are among St. Thomas' most popular tourist attractions.

Congo Cay 2

Typical Depth Range:	29-90 feet
Typical Current Conditions:	Generally less than one-half knot
Expertise Required:	Novice with instructor or divemaster
Access:	Boat

About three miles northeast of St. John is Congo Cay, a dive area visited by dive operators from both St. Thomas and St. John. It is part of a series of small islets or cays that extend between the two large islands. Located near Carval Rock, it is a 30-minute boat ride from St. John and only slightly longer from St. Thomas.

The conditions here are generally manageable and dive boats tend to anchor on the south side of the island in the lee. Unlike Carval Rock, which juts farther into Pillsbury Sound, Congo Cay's location offers more protection from the tidal flow and subsequent currents, which can become excessive at Carval Rock.

Congo Cay is distinguished by its reefs, rocks and boulders. Between 30 and 60 feet, divers will find the most marine activity. A series of seamounts off the west end of the island provides a vibrantly colored tapestry, ideal for photographers. You will find some of the best photo opportunities between 20 and 40 feet. The northern side of the Cay plunges to 75 feet, where lobsters hide among large boulders and the chances of spotting eagle rays, tarpon, and even manta rays are good.

Divers cruise among the large coral and sponge encrusted formations like those found at Congo Cay.

On the southern end of the island, a rock wall drops vertically to anywhere from 225 to 300 feet, but there really is not much to see beyond about 90 feet. The nicest spot for divers to explore is around the 50-foot mark where there seems to be a lot of marine activity. Manta rays and eagle rays have been seen frequently in this area so keep an eye out. Look above you and out into the deeper water for dark shapes in the distance. It is amazing how many divers miss out on some of the most exciting creatures swimming just above them because they are looking in only one direction! You are also likely to see tarpon and an occasional blacktip reef shark at this site.

This is also a great spot to see a diverse array of invertebrates that make their home on the rocks. Orange tubastrea carpets the rock faces and, at night, explodes in full bloom to create a spectacular tangerine-hued garden.

Tubastrea flourishes on the reefs at night at Congo Cay.

Typical Depth Range:	55 feet maximum
Typical Current Conditions:	Light to moderate current
Expertise Required:	Novice
Access:	Boat

Although Grass Cay is located only 10 minutes by boat from the dock at Stouffer Grand Beach Hotel on St. Thomas, the site attracts dive operators from St. John as well. The dive area, which is situated in a sandy anchorage on the south side of Grass Cay, is one of those places to which divers like to return.

The dive begins fairly shallow at about 20 feet. From 20 to 50 feet, the terrain is a variegated carpet of densely packed coral that conceals a plethora of surprises at a distance. But upon closer observation, the coral heads reveal an abundance of invertebrate life from dainty Christmas tree worms and featherdusters to bristle worms and tunicates.

Large sea fans sway almost imperceptibly because there is generally little or no current, which also contributes to the above average visibility. There is no shortage, of fish life either. Chromis, hamlets, grunts, creole wrasse, trunk fish, and large hermit crabs inhabit this territory. Barracuda cruise by regularly. In the summertime, turtle encounters are not unusual. This dive site has some of the best hard coral formations in the area.

Grass Cay abounds with delicate featherduster worms.

The camera captures the eye of a conch that peeks tentatively from its shell at Grass Cay.

Typical Depth Range: 45 feet maximum
Typical Current Conditions: Surge, pay attention
Expertise Required: Novice with instructor or divemaster
Access: Boat

Just off the northwest point of Thatch Cay is a dive site considered by some divers to be the "piece de resistance" of dive sites — Tunnels of Thatch Cay. A relatively shallow dive averaging about 40 feet, it is an easy but wonderfully varied underwater experience to be enjoyed by all levels of divers. It is recommended that novices be accompanied by a divemaster or instructor only because the surge can be difficult to negotiate at times, especially for less experienced individuals.

The Tunnels is visited by dive operators from both St. John and St. Thomas so no matter where you are based, you will have the opportunity to explore this site. The bottom terrain is rocky, distinguished by a series

Blue tangs like this one found at Thatch Cay are challenges for underwater photographers because they are constantly in motion.

Orange cup corals shroud the overhangs and tunnels that punctuate the dive sites around Thatch Cay.

of canyons and passageways. Seven arches and tunnels challenge the imagination of divers. Although most of the tunnels are short in length, one tunnel is a 60-foot, dog-legged passageway where divers enter on the bay side and emerge on the ocean side. Another square-shaped tunnel, which is somewhat protected from the surge, reveals bright orange tubastrea and delicate black coral.

The high level of ambient light and the diversity and dramatic sculpturing of the terrain make this an excellent dive for underwater photography. For fish portraits or wide-angle photography, you will find tarpon, especially during the summer months, a host of tropical fish, expansive clouds of silversides, and interesting coral formations including the highly photogenic pillar coral.

Clearly, variety is the spice of this dive, which local dive operators rank with the best of them. It is not only a favorite of divemasters but of divers as well.

Divers should note that, while this is not a difficult dive, the surge can on occasion become exceptionally heavy in the winter months. Pay extra attention to ensure that you do not inadvertently bang against the fragile corals and sponges that help to make this dive such a special one.

59

Typical Depth Range:	42 to 62 feet
Typical Current Conditions:	Can get very heavy current; there is a mooring on the site
Expertise Required:	Intermediate
Access:	Boat

Located almost directly in front of one of the most delightful resorts in St. Thomas, Stouffers Grand Beach Resort, is the wreck of the *Major General Rogers*. A 120-foot, steel-hulled, self-propelled auxiliary Coast Guard vessel, it was probably in service as a buoy tender as evidenced by large reels on its stern. In l972, the *Major General Rogers* was intentionally sunk by the Department of Planning and Natural Resources to create an artificial reef. It now rests upright, its wheelhouse missing, in 42 to 65 feet of clear, fish-filled water in the windward passage.

Marine life is abundant and flourishing on this wreck. Tube sponges, hard and soft corals, purple tunicates, curling hydroids and striped bristleworms provide splashes of color all over the gray hulk. Within the confines of her open cargo holds and around the hull, pompano, Spanish hogfish, and schools of grunts and snapper circle rhythmically. Curious barracuda hover silently nearby.

This is an ideal dive site for all types of photography whether you want to concentrate on macro, fish portraits, or wide angle. Macro enthusiasts should look for the many colonies of vibrant purple tunicates and

The prop of the Major General Rogers *is thickly encrusted with a tapestry of colorful corals and sponges.*

Brilliant purple tunicate colonies are scattered over the deck and sides of the wreck of the Major General Rogers.

bristleworms that abound. The porthole on the starboard stern and color-fully encrusted propeller make excellent subjects for wide angle photographers.

About 200 feet from the *General Rogers* is a second wreck. This vessel, which was sunk at about the same time as the *General Rogers* is an overturned self-propelled Coast Guard barge. It is not recommended for divers to swim inside because the interior is very cramped and silty. A line attaches the two wrecks and they can be explored on the same dive. However, the *General Rogers* has so much to offer that it is likely divers will expend their bottom time without ever leaving this wreck.

Coki Beach

If you're looking for a good place to snorkel on St. Thomas, Coki Beach is one place to check out. It is located adjacent to Coral World and its easy beach access has made it one of the island's most popular areas for snorkeling and for resort course diving.

It is also a good place for an early morning or night dive on scuba. At Coki Reef which slopes to 60 feet, early risers can capture the sunrise activity of the reef as it slowly comes to life with the dawning day. At night, after the cruise ship passengers and Coral World visitors have departed, the nocturnal reef blooms with vibrant color and marine creatures from small invertebrates to tarpon, rays, octopus, and luminescent Atlantic oval squid enjoy the tranquility of the evening solitude. It is an ideal spot to try your new camera or video equipment!

There are picnic tables conveniently placed near the beach and you can buy refreshments at the nearby food stand. It's an ideal place to stop for a very casual bite at lunchtime . . . and maybe a quick dip to cool off after a morning of hot sightseeing!

Coki Beach is a popular spot for snorkeling, night diving, and sunworshipping.

Cruise ships brings passengers to Coki Beach for scuba diving resort courses.

Ledges of Little St. James 6

Typical Depth Range:	15-40 feet
Typical Current Conditions:	Almost always calm
Expertise Required:	Novice
Access:	Boat

Besides being owned by multi-millionaire and cosmetic mogul Charles Revson, who built his fame and financial empire with Revlon Cosmetics, Little St. James is an unusual island. Located on the southwest side of the island is a unusual dive site with huge, deeply indented ledges and prolific tropical marine life. It is ideal for the novice diver because it is well-protected from currents or surge and offers a maximum depth of only 40 feet.

The most interesting features of the dive can be experienced to the fullest in depths from 15 to 25 feet. Within this shallow range, you will find several exquisite stands of pillar coral including one that majestically looms at 8 to 10 feet tall. The deep undercuts for which the dive site derives its name reveal a variegated patchwork of encrusting corals. Nearby boulders are similarly encrusted with coral from which colorful

63

Little St. James' many ledges and overhangs display a kaleidoscope of colorful coral and sponges.

◀ *Elegant stands of pillar coral are among the distinctive features of the dive site at Ledges of Little St. James.*

Christmas tree worms and fragile featherdusters timidly emerge and retract. Beware of the mustard brown fire coral and the occasional black sea urchin!

There is no shortage of marine activity. If you have the patience of a saint, a circling juvenile spotted drum may permit you to take a photo. Porcupine fish, lobster, schooling grunts, big lizardfish, as well as queen and gray angels are among the permanent residents in the area.

This is also a superb night dive. The water is generally calm. The color is vibrant. You will find it quite easy to find wonderful creatures all over the site. This is a must for macro photography.

Typical Depth Range:	25-40 feet
Typical Current Conditions:	Generally no current; frequent surge action
Expertise Required:	Novice with instructor or divemaster
Access:	Boat

If you head off the southeast end of St. Thomas, you will come upon some rocks that barely break the surface of the water. As legend goes, the larger of the rocks were mistakenly identified by a nearsighted mariner as migrating humpback whales, a cow and her calf.

At the west end of "the cow," there is an H-shaped network of coral tunnels that is roomy enough to accommodate two divers. Inside the tunnels, with the aide of a dive light, you'll see the rough-hewn walls transform into a kaleidoscope of dazzling colors as the red encrusting corals, yellow sponges and orange tubastrea come to life. Even though

A diver swims through a submerged tunnel at Cow and Calf Rocks.

this particular site has little silt to stir up, be careful not to kick up the bottom so divers who swim through after you can enjoy the experience as well.

In addition to the tunnels, archways, overhangs, and undercuts enhance the beauty and excitement of this dive. Copper sweepers can be found in the rear of one of the overhangs, which also has a small outlet to the surface. You are likely to encounter schools of horse-eye jacks that cruise the periphery of the rocks. You may even see a nurse shark resting quietly under one of the ledges or near the base of the rocks as it oxygenates its gills in the moving water. The arches, in particular, offer some excellent opportunities for wide-angle photography.

This is an ideal spot for the curious diver. With a maximum depth around 40 feet, you are unlikely to run out nooks and crannies to explore before you run out of bottom time.

This is not a particularly deep dive, but it is generally recommended as an intermediate dive due to the surge conditions. For divers with some experience, this is simply an inconvenience.

A red fan worm like this one found at Cow and Calf Rocks is a member of the Serpulidae *family, which includes all tube-dwelling creatures.*

Typical Depth Range:	30-70 feet
Typical Current Conditions:	Generally none
Expertise Required:	Novice (under ideal conditions) to intermediate
Access:	Boat

   Located approximately 2.5 miles south of St. Thomas, Capella Island is one of the more accessible sites from St. Thomas. On the southeast side of the island is Capella Reef, a sloping terrain well endowed with marine activity.

   The diving is at its best from 40 to 80 feet. Because visibility is generally quite good, averaging about 80 feet, divers can almost be assured of a clear view of the seascape.

   Approaching the sea floor, divers will see enormous blocks of igneous rock lying at various tilts and angles, forming a series of oversized ravines through which divers can swim and explore.

   There is ample growth on the reef, dominated by colorful encrusting corals of many varieties. Pillar coral, one of nature's most beautiful and dramatic gifts to the sea environment, can be seen here. Be careful not to touch or brush against this very fragile coral as it is fairly rare. Hard

Large blocks of igneous rock form oversized ravines through which divers can swim at Capella Island.

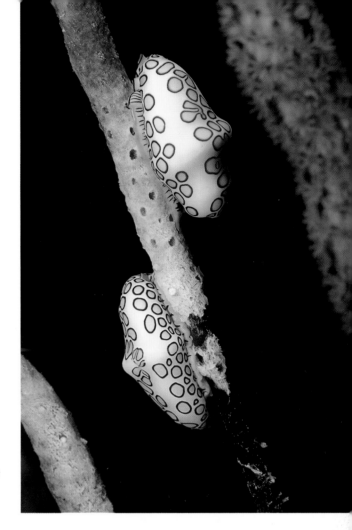

Flamingo tongues feed on soft coral polyps of soft corals that can be on the dive sites throughout the U.S. Virgin Islands.

corals are frequently adorned by seawhips and lavender sea fans that sway hypnotically with the imperceptible current.

The marine life on the reef is accustomed to divers and you will find them to be friendly and approachable. Photographers will appreciate the reliable appearance of French and queen angelfish, which make ideal models for fish portraits. Here is where patience and persistence are invaluable assets! This area also attracts a prolific community of blue chromis.

Although this is one of the few dive sites that experienced serious and extensive damage when Hurricane Hugo swept through the U.S. Virgin Islands in 1989, the coral has begun to regenerate well and the site is still a very pretty dive.

Novice divers who want to experience this dive should make sure the conditions are at their best — calm seas, no current, and good visibility. If the water conditions are not ideal, ask the divemaster or instructor to accompany you on the dive.

Submarine Atlantis

Whether you're a scuba diver or not, the world of Jacques Cousteau holds a fascination for all of us. But you don't necessarily have to don tanks or a snorkel or even get your feet wet to see what all the excitement is about. All you have to do is step aboard the submarine *Atlantis* in St. Thomas for a voyage beneath the sea. *Atlantis'* one-hour cruise promises to be an incredible adventure of discovery during which you experience the wonders of the marine environment of the Caribbean.

Advanced design and space-age technology enables this air-conditioned, high-tech mini-sub to carry 46 passengers and three crew members to depths of up to 150 feet where colorful and exotic sea life, sponge gardens, unusual marine creatures, and coral formations appear larger than life. A crew member guides you through the journey with an informative narration of what you are seeing as you move through the water.

The *Atlantis* is 65 feet long and 13 feet wide and travels at 1.5 knots underwater. Twenty-six large viewports, each two feet in diameter, and an oversized 52-inch front viewport enable passengers an unobstructed panorama. For night dives, the vessel is equipped with 12 floodlights in addition to normal navigational lights so you won't miss a splash of color or a nocturnal creature!

Atlantis operates seven days a week and reservations are recommended. For information, contact Atlantis III, Bldg. VI, Havensight Mall, St. Thomas, U.S.V.I., 00802, 809-776-5650.

The Wreck of the *Cartanser Senior* 9

Typical Depth Range:	25-35 feet
Typical Current Conditions:	None
Expertise Required:	Novice
Access:	Boat

According to various versions of *Cartanser Senior*'s demise, the 190-foot steel-hulled freighter had served to transport goods during World War II. Later it operated as an inter-island freighter, and rumor has it that its cargo was not altogether legal. It was eventually deserted by its

Decorative Christmas tree worms compete for space with orange cup coral on the wreck of the Cartanser Senior.

A French angelfish cruises near the bottom of the wreck of the Cartanser Senior.

captain and crew for reasons that may or may not be a mystery. Abandoned and unmanned, it began to take on water and ultimately sunk in the Gregerie Channel in St. Thomas harbor.

As the Corps of Engineers prepared to destroy the vessel, which presented a clear navigational hazard, an underwater picket line of divers successfully intervened to preserve their "dive site." *Cartanser Senior* was relocated to the west side of Buck Island. A few years later, Hurricane Alan saw to it that the wreck was relocated once again.

Cartanser Senior now rests on its port side in 35 to 50 feet of water, its hull split into three sections. Divers can safely swim through its holds and bulkhead hatches to explore the cargo areas, engine room, and various parts of the vessel's interior.

With the help of daily fish feeding by local divemasters, the wreck attracts a significant fish population. Sergeant majors, parrotfish, angelfish, and yellowtail snappers are only a few of the species that frequent the premises of this wreck. The wreck is well-encrusted with sponges and corals. If you swim to the stern and look beneath the flare where there is little light, you can see orange tubastrea in full bloom, a delight at night and a rare sight during the day.

This dive is ideal for a first wreck dive or for the novice diver. Situated in a well-protected cove, there are no heavy currents or surge on this wreck. Visibility is generally good so divers can view a large portion of the wreck at one time. It is no wonder that *Cartanser Senior* is one of the most popular dives in St. Thomas.

Typical Depth Range:	40-75 feet
Typical Current Conditions:	Slight, mild current
Expertise Required:	Intermediate to advanced
Access:	Boat

Only 25 minutes from Compass Point in Charlotte Amalie and 40 minutes from East End, French Cap Cay lies off the southern shore of St. Thomas. From a distance it can be seen rising from the sea, stark, dark, and imposing. This dive area is better suited to divers with some experience due to the depth of the dive. Off the northeast part of French Cap Cay is a dive site called Deep Ledges, aptly named for considerable indentations that distinguish the terrain. The ledge area begin at about 40 feet, dropping sharply to 75 feet and running more than 300 feet in length. Deep ledges cut dramatically into the rocks as deeply as 20 to 25 feet, roomy enough for divers to explore. One area has a hole at the top large enough for divers to swim through.

While the terrain of this site creates an exciting dive, the marine life is equally compelling. Curious barracuda, sennets, queen and French angelfish, and groupers are often joined by more illusive creatures such spotted eagle rays, octopus, nurse sharks, and oversized hawksbill turtles.

One of the special charms of this site is the excellent visibility that sometimes reaches as much as 200 feet!

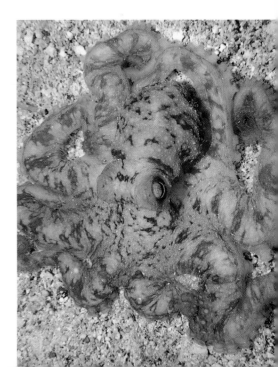

A chance encounter with a three-inch juvenile octopus is one of the experiences that makes French Cap Cay an exciting dive area.

It is not uncommon to find a curious barracuda observing divers at close range at French Cap Cay.

Typical Depth Range:	45-95 feet
Typical Current Conditions:	½ knot is common, almost always rough
Expertise Required:	Intermediate and up
Access:	Boat

Not too far from the southern tip of French Cap Cay is a small seamount called the Pinnacle. The boat ride to French Cap Cay is an hour or longer and most diver operators will do a second, shallower dive at another French Cap Cay site.

The pinnacle begins in 45 feet of water. Photographs of the two stone monoliths that adorn the summit of the seamount have graced the pages of numerous dive publications. Due to the typically excellent visibility, divers can see the entire seamount from the surface when they enter the water.

Schools of fish play among the two rocks and there is a good chance that you may see eagle rays gracefully gliding around the Pinnacle if you are among the first divers in the water.

Divers should keep a sharp eye out for eagle rays that are occasionally spotted at the Pinnacle at French Cap Cay.

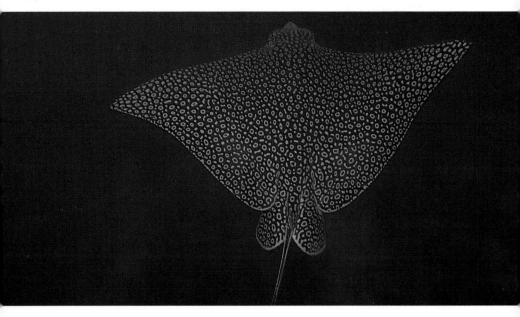

Stoplight parrotfish, like this one found at the Pinnacle at French Cap Cay, are common on all the dive sites around the U.S. Virgin Islands.

Between 50 and 80 feet, a leisurely series of circuits around the Pinnacle reveals shapely and colorful barrel and tube sponges. If you have a camera with you, take advantage of the clear water and the unique structure of the pinnacle itself. Choose a subject such as a sponge, and shoot upward toward the surface. If the dive boat is moored over the Pinnacle which is often the case, including the silhouette of the boat in the photo will create a dramatic effect. The base of the Pinnacle sits at 90 to 95 feet on the ocean bottom.

You will rarely be disappointed by the visibility. It has been described by more than one experienced diver as spectacular. If you have never dived a seamount before, this is one of the best examples on which to take the plunge!

Because there is no shallow reef to explore around the Pinnacle, most dive operators will try to put divers in the water as close to it as possible. In the event that there is more than a little current, remember to swim into the current at the beginning of the dive so that you don't have to fight it when you are returning to the boat with less energy and less air.

Typical Depth Range:	20-50 feet
Typical Current Conditions:	None, some surge action with weather
Expertise Required:	Intermediate
Access:	Boat

A 25-minute boat ride southwest of Charlotte Amalie will bring you to Saba Island. If you have had the opportunity to dive Capella Island, you will find that the underwater terrain on the southeast reef is a smaller scale version. Sizable rock boulders are scattered on the seafloor at 50 feet. Divers will discover a natural archway at 30 to 40 feet, one of the distinguishing landmarks of this site.

In the shallower areas where the rock facades are gently washed by the surge, small but dramatic stands of staghorn coral thrive. Divers may also see some good examples of pillar coral. Creole wrasse seem to be attracted to this spot in quantity, easily identified by their intense deep blue coloring and spotty facial markings. Rock beauties make stunning subjects for fish portraits and they, too, can always be seen swimming amid the coral heads. Be patient if you are trying to photograph them. They tend to be a bit elusive as they wend their way through nooks and

Attentive divers may be lucky enough to find an elusive juvenile spotted drum around Saba Island.

Despite any damage caused by Hurricane Hugo in 1989, fast growing corals such as staghorn coral, regenerated quickly on many of the dive sites throughout the U.S. Virgin Islands.

crannies inaccessible to your camera but the bright yellow and black contrast of their bodies makes an excellent photo. Angelfish can also found cruising slowly nearby.

Although the staghorn coral loves the surge, it can be troublesome for divers, especially where there is fire coral. Just in case there is surge on the day you dive this site, bring along a wetsuit or skin that affords some protection. Coral scrapes and stings are not dangerous, but they are decidedly unpleasant! Practicing proper buoyancy control will save both you and the reef from damage.

Wreck of RMS Rhone

Without question, one of the most famous Caribbean shipwrecks is the *RMS Rhone*. It is a truly dramatic wreck, invariably a favorite. And, although the wreck of the *Rhone* officially lies within the waters of the British Virgin Islands, dive operators from St. Thomas do include it in their dive itinerary, some as frequently as once a week.

A former 350-foot British Royal Mail Steamer built in 1865, the *RMS Rhone* sunk only two years later when a hurricane cast her onto the rocks at Salt Island. Today, more than a century and a quarter later, she is most famous for her starring role in the movie, *The Deep*. The wreck of the *Rhone* lies in three sections and at least 100 feet of the original structure remains intact. The bow complete with bowsprit and foremast lies on its starboard side.

At night the bow section, which lies in 70 to 80 feet of water, is a symphony of orange tubastrea corals, vibrantly colored encrusting sponges, elusive orange ball anemones, and basketstars. The center section at 40 to 70 feet is a labyrinth of deck beams, which are reminiscent of ancient Greek columns encrusted with a rainbow of sponges and soft and hard corals.

Swimming along the shaft through the gear box in the stern section, you might encounter a fearless sergeant major who has made this his (or her) home. A sizable green moray eel hangs out on the bow. In less than 25 feet of water, her rudder and propeller can be seen lying amid her shattered aft section.

If you have the opportunity to dive this wreck, it is well worth the all-day trip. You can do numerous dives on this remnant of antiquity and every one will be a fresh experience.

Nearby, only a short swim from the wreck of the *Rhone* is Rhone Reef. The reef breaks the surface where waves break against the towering rocks and then drops to about 40 feet of water. You can explore three caves that are fairly close together and are usually filled with schools of copper sweepers. There are some nice photo subjects here . . . but none that compare to those on the wreck!

The dramatic wreck of the Rhone, *which sunk in 1867, is frequently visited by dive operators from St. Thomas and St. John.*

5

Smart, Safe Diving

Preparation

Before you leave home, make sure all of your dive gear is in good working order and that all items that must be serviced yearly — especially regulators — have been. There is nothing as aggravating as getting on the boat, arriving on your first dive site, only to discover that your octopus is free-flowing. If you wear a mask with a prescription or have trouble finding a mask that fits you correctly, bring a backup mask. Masks have been known to arrive at a different destination that you, fall overboard, or break. You won't be comfortable with a borrowed mask if you can't see or if it keeps leaking. Finally, if you haven't been diving for 6 months or more, especially if you have logged fewer than 20 dives, it might be a good idea take a practice or refresher dive either in a local pool at home or with an instructor at a dive store in the islands before you head for deep water.

Reef Etiquette and Buoyancy Control

While moorings may go a long way toward reducing anchor damage to our reefs, so far there is nothing to protect them from damage by divers . . . except divers. Dive sites tend to be located where the reefs and walls display the most beautiful corals and sponges. And it only takes a moment — an inadvertently placed hand or knee on the coral or an unaware brush or kick with a fin — to destroy this fragile living part of our delicate ecosystem. Only a moment to make dive site a little less spectacular for other divers. Luckily, it only takes a little extra preparation and consideration to preserve it for generations of divers to come.

So if you're a new diver, a little rusty after a long hiatus on dry land, diving with new equipment . . . or if you just haven't paid much attention to your reef etiquette and buoyancy control in the past, here are a few helpful tips how you can personally help preserve our underwater environment:

Weight Yourself Properly. Never dive with too much weight. (Northern divers — this means you! When you put on a lighter wetsuit or dive skin, shed some of those lead pounds, too!) Weight yourself so that you *float at eye level* on the surface with your lungs full of air and none in your BCD. Exhale fully and you should begin to sink. As your week of diving goes by and you relax underwater, drop some more weight. Ask your divemaster what kind of tank you're using. Tanks vary in their buoyancy when they are empty. You want to able to hover comfortably at 15 feet to make your safety stop when your tank is low at the end of your dive.

Control Your Buoyancy with Your Breathing. If you are properly weighted and have successfully attained neutral buoyancy with your BCD. at depth, you should be able to fine-tune your hovering capacity by inhaling and exhaling. Being able to rise and sink at will is the real trick to being able to hover, float, and glide over and around the reef formations with grace and skill.

Avoid Fin Damage to Coral. Never stand (or kneel) on the corals. If you're hovering above the reef, keep your fins up off the reef. If you're swimming, do so in a horizontal position looking down so you're not flutter-kicking the reef. When you're cruising through a narrow space such as a tunnel or gully between coral heads, keep an eye on where your feet are and, if necessary, make your kick small and efficient to move you through the compact area. Reef etiquette also demands that, if your are swimming near a sandy bottom, stay several feet above the sand so you don't kick up any silt and ruin the dive for other divers.

Don't Touch the Reef. No matter how pretty and tactile the coral and sponges are, look but don't touch. And never, never grab onto the reef to steady yourself. If you need to stabilize yourself or keep from bumping into things or other divers, try using one or two fingers instead of your entire hand. And look for dead spots, areas between the corals or even the underside of a coral cranny where there is generally less growth.

Watch Where You Land. If you need to touch down or kneel on solid ground, look for a sandy area in between the coral heads. If you need to take a photo, float or glide over your subject or steady yourself with a finger, but keep the rest of your body away from the reef. If you can't get the picture or see your subject without lying on the coral . . . don't take the picture!

A diver observes proper "reef etiquette" by hovering well above the reef and looking but not touching the delicate sponges and corals.

Don't Drag Loose Gauges or Octopus Across the Reef. Hanging consoles, goody bags, tools, and other unsecured equipment can do as much damage to the corals as your hands and feet. Keep your equipment close to your body by tucking them into your BC pockets or using retainer clips. You can even put your console between your tank and your back.

Don't Grab the Marine Creatures. Don't ride the turtles, grab the lobsters, chase the stingrays or harass the eels. They are curious by nature and will gradually move toward you if you leave them alone. If you grab them, they'll disappear faster than you can clear your mask . . . and no one else will have the chance to see them either.

Be considerate. Leave the reef in the same condition in which you find. In this way, it will remain healthy and thriving for future divers to enjoy.

Hazardous Marine Life

Diving in the U.S.V.I.'s isn't really hazardous. It's divers who are hazardous. When was the last time a stand of fire coral pursued a diver to sting him? Most stings, scrapes, and punctures are due to divers inadvertently bumping into coral or touching a creature that instinctively defends itself against its giant aggressor. Some are harmless and merely uncomfortable. Others may require medical attention. Ideally, we shouldn't be touching anything underwater, but it does happen and it does hurt!

Watch out for the following:

Fire Coral. Mustard brown in color, fire coral is most often found in shallower waters encrusting dead gorgonians or coral. Contact causes a burning sensation that lasts for several minutes and sometimes causes red welts on the skin. If you rub against fire coral, do not try to rub the affected area as you will spread the small stinging particles. Upon resurfacing, apply meat tenderizer to relieve the sting and then antibiotic cream. Cortisone cream can also reduce any inflammation.

Sponges. They may be beautiful, but sponges can also pack a powerful punch with fine spicules that sting on contact. While bright reddish brown ones are often the stinging kind, familiarly called "dread red," they are not the only culprits. If you touch a stinging sponge, scrape the area with the edge of your dive knife. Home remedies include mild vinegar or ammonia solutions to ease the pain, but most of it will subside within a day. Again, cortisone cream might help.

Sea Urchins. The urchin's most dangerous weapon is its spines, which can penetrate neoprene wetsuits, booties, and gloves with ease. You'll know you've been jabbed from the instant pain. Urchins tend to be more common in shallow areas near shore and come out of their shelters under coral heads at night. If you are beach diving, beware of urchins that may be lying on the shallow reef you have to cross to reach deeper water. Don't move across it on your hands and knees and start swimming as soon as possible. Injuries should be attended to as soon as possible because infection can occur. Minor punctures require removal of the spine and treatment with an antibiotic cream. More serious ones should be looked at by a doctor.

◀ *Proper buoyancy control will enable a diver to swim comfortably along the reef without bumping or kicking the coral.*

Bristle Worms. Bristle worms make a great subject for macro photography but don't touch them to move them to the perfect spot. Use a strobe arm or dive knife. Contact will result in tiny stinging bristles being embedded in the skin and resulting in a burning feeling or welt. You can try to scrape the bristles off with the edge of a dive knife. Otherwise, they will work themselves out within a few days. Again, cortisone cream can help minimize any inflammation.

Sea Wasps. A possibly serious diving hazard, sea wasps are small, potent jellyfish with four stinging tentacles and they generally swim within a few feet of the surface at night. If sea wasps have been spotted in the water where you are planning to do a night dive, take caution. Don't linger on the surface upon entry into the water. When you return, turn your dive light off as it attracts them and exit the water as quickly as possible. Their sting is very painful and leaves a red welt as a reminder. *Do not* try to push them away from your area of ascent by sending air bubbles to the surface from your regulator. The bubbles may break off their tentacles and you won't be able to see where the stinging tentacles are. If you are allergic to bee stings, and sea wasps have been spotted at the dive site, consider foregoing the dive as you will most likely have the same reaction to a sea wasp sting.

Stonefish. They may be one of the sea's best camouflaged creatures, but if you receive a puncture by the poisonous spines that are hidden among its fins, you'll know you've found a stonefish. They tend to lie on the bottom or on coral, so, unless your are lying on the bottom or on the reef — which you shouldn't be (see "Reef Etiquette and Buoyancy Control"), they shouldn't present a problem. Should you get stung, go to a hospital or a doctor as soon as possible because it can result in severe allergic reactions, and pain and infection are almost guaranteed.

Stingrays. These guys are harmless unless you sit or step on them. If you harass them, you may discover the long, barbed stinger which is located at the base of the tail and wields a very painful wound that can be deep and become infected. If you suffer from a sting, go to a hospital or seek a doctor's care immediately. But the best policy is to leave them alone, and they'll leave you alone in return.

Eels. Similarly, eels won't bother you unless you bother them. It is best not to hand feed them, especially when you don't know if other eels or hazardous fish such as barracudas or sharks are in the area. And don't put your hand in a dark hole because it might just house an eel. Eels have extremely poor eyesight and cannot always distinguish between food and your hand. If you are bitten by an eel, don't try to pull your hand away — their teeth are extraordinary sharp. Let the eel release it and then surface (at the required slow rate of ascent), apply first aid, and then head for the nearest hospital.

Sharks. Though not an extremely common sight for divers, when sharks do appear, it is a cause for celebration and fascination. As a rule, most of the sharks you will encounter in the U.S. Virgin Islands are not aggressive and will not attack divers. However, it is wise not to feed them or harass them. If you are unlucky enough to be mistaken for a meal, the nearest hospital is the most logical next stop.

Barracuda. Barracudas have a miserable reputation. In fact, they are somewhat shy, although unnervingly curious. They will hover near enough to divers to observe what they are so interested in, but just try to photograph them and they keep their distance. You'll see them on almost every dive. Don't bother them, and they'll not bother you.

Diving Accidents

Diving is a safe sport and there are very few accidents compared to the number of divers and dives made each year. However, occasionally accidents do occur and emergency medical treatment should be sought immediately. If you are diving with a local dive operation on one of the U.S. Virgin Islands, they will be equipped to handle any situation expediently. If a diving injury or decompression sickness occurs when you are on your own, here are some important *emergency numbers* to contact:

St. Croix Hospital	778-6311
St. John (Morris de Castro) Clinic	776-6400
St. Thomas Hospital	776-8311
Ambulance service	922
Air Ambulance (St. Thomas)	772-1629/778-9200
U.S. Coast Guard	774-1911
Recompression Chamber (St. Thomas)	776-2686
Divers Alert Network	(919) 684-8111

Divers Alert Network/DAN. The Divers Alert Network (DAN), a non-profit membership association of individuals and organizations sharing a common interest in diving safety, assists in the treatment of underwater diving accidents by operating a 24-hour national telephone emergency hotline, **(919) 684-8111** (collect calls are accepted), and to increase diver safety awareness through education.

DAN does *not* maintain any treatment facility nor does it directly provide any form of treatment, but is a service that complements existing medical systems. DAN's most important function is facilitating the entry of the injured diver into the hyperbaric trauma care system by coordinating the efforts of everyone involved in the victim's care.

Calls for routine information that do not concern a suspected diving injury or emergency should be directed to DAN information number (919) 684-2948 from 9 a.m. and 5 p.m. Monday - Friday Eastern Standard time. This number should *not* be called for general information of chamber locations. Chamber availability changes periodically making obsolete information dangerous at the time of an emergency. Instead, divers should contact DAN as soon as a diving emergency is suspected.

Hyperbaric treatment and air ambulance service can be costly. All divers who have comprehensive medical insurance should check to make sure that hyperbaric treatment and air ambulance services are adequately covered internationally. DAN membership includes insurance coverage specifically for dive injuries. Four different membership levels offering four different levels of coverage are available.

DAN provides diving safety information to members to help prevent accidents. Membership ranges from $25-45 a year, which includes dive accident insurance, the *DAN Underwater Diving Accident Manual*, which summarizes each type of major diving injury and outlines procedures for initial management and care of the victim; a membership card listing diving related symptoms and DAN's emergency and non-emergency phone numbers; decals with DAN's logo and emergency number; and *Alert Diver*, a newsletter that provides information on diving medicine and safety in layman's language. Special memberships for dive stores, dive clubs, and corporations are available. The DAN Manual as well as membership information and applications can be obtained from the Administrative Coordinator, National Diving Alert Network, Duke University Medical Center, Box 3823, Durham, NC 27710.

When the infrequent injury does occur, DAN is prepared to help. DAN support currently comes from diver membership and contributions from the diving industry. It is a legal non-profit public service organization and all donations are tax deductible.

Appendix 1: Dive Operations

This list is included as a service to the reader. The publisher has made every effort to make this list accurate at the time the book was printed. This list does not constitute an endorsement of these operators and dive shops. If operators/owners wish to be included in future reprints/editions, please contact Pisces Books, P.O. Box 2608, Houston, Texas 77252-2608.

St. Thomas

Aqua Action Dive Center
Red Hook, St. Thomas 00802
809-775-6285

Caribbean Divers
Red Hook, St. Thomas 00802
809-775-6384

Chris Sawyer Dive Center
Compass Point Marina, St. Thomas
  00802
809-775-7320

Chris Sawyer Dive Center
Stouffer Grand Beach Resort
Smith Bay, St. Thomas
809-775-1510 ext.7850

Coki Beach Dive Club
P.O. Box 5279
Coki Beach, St. Thomas 00803
809-771-2343

Dive In!
Sapphire Beach Marina,
  St. Thomas 00803
809-775-6100/800-524-2040

Joe Vogel Diving Co.
West Indies Inn, Frenchtown,
  Box 7322, St. Thomas 00801
809-775-7610/800-448-6224

St. Thomas Diving Club
Bolongo Bay Beach Resort, Box 7337
St. Thomas 00801
809-775-1800/800-524-4746

Underwater Safaris, Inc.
Ramada Yacht Haven
St. Thomas 00801
809-774-1350

V.I. Diving Schools Inc.
P.O. Box 9707
Vitraco Park, St. Thomas 00801
809-774-8687

Hi-Tech Watersports
P.O. Box 2180
Frenchtown, St. Thomas 00803
809-774-5650

Paradise Watersports
P.O. Box 57
Red Hook, St. Thomas 00802
809-776-7618

Ocean Quest Divers
P.O. Box 3184
Benner Bay, St. Thomas 00803
809-776-5176/800-524-2130

Ocean Fantasies
Box 9544
Windward Hotel, St. Thomas 00801
809-774-5223

St. John

Cinnamon Bay Watersports
Cinnamon Bay Beach
Cinnamon Bay, St. John 00830
809-776-6330

Low Key Watersports
P.O. Box 431
Wharfside, St. John 00831
809-776-7048

Paradise Watersports
Caneel Bay Resort
Caneel Bay, St. John 00830
809-776-7618

St. John Watersports
P.O. Box 70
Cruz Bay, St. John 00831
809-776-6256

St. Croix

Blue Paradise Scuba
Carambola Beach Resort
Davis Bay, St. Croix 00851
809-778-3598

Cruzan Divers
12 Strand Street
Frederiksted, St. Croix 00840
800-247-8186/809-772-3701

Dive Experience
P.O. Box 4254
1 Strand Street
Christiansted, St. Croix 00822
800-235-9047/809-773-3307

Dive St. Croix
59 Kings Wharf
Christiansted, St. Croix 00820
809-773-3434/800-523-DIVE

Mile Mark Watersports
59 King's Wharf
Christiansted, St. Croix 00820
809-773-2628/809-773-3434

Sea Horse Watersports
Box 2561
Frederiksted, St. Croix 00822
809-772-5552

Underwater St. Croix
Box 261266, G. Bay
Green Cay Marina, St. Croix 00824
809-778-7350

V.I. Divers Ltd.
Pan Am Pavilion
Christiansted, St. Croix 00820
809-773-6045/800-544-5911

Appendix 2: Further Reading

Barnes, Robert D., *Invertebrate Zoology*, Saunders College/Holt, Rinehart and Winston, Philadelphia, Pa., 1980.

Colin, P., *Caribbean Reef Invertebrates and Plants*, T.F.H. Publishing Co., Neptune City, N.J., 1987.

Greenberg, I. and J., *Waterproof Guide to Corals and Fishes*, Seahawk Press, Miami, Fl., 1977.

Humann, Paul, *Reef Fish Identification*, Vaughan Press, Orlando, Fl. 1989.

Humfrey, Michael, *Sea Shells of the West Indies*, Collins, London, England, 1975.

Kaplan, Eugene H., *A Field Guide to Coral Reefs*, Houghton Mifflin Company, Boston, Ma. 1982.

Meinkoth, Norman A., *The Audubon Society Field Guide to North American Seashore Creatures*, Knopf, New York, N.Y., 1981.

Pisces Photo Pak® of Caribbean Reef Fish, Pisces Books, Houston, Texas, 1990.

Wilson R. and J., *Pisces Guide to Watching Fishes: Understanding Coral Reef Fish Behavior*, Pisces Books, Houston, Texas, 1985/1992.

Index

Boldface page numbers include photograph(s) of subject.